‹ WEST BANK/ GAZA STRIP ›

WEST BANK/ GAZA STRIP

Rebecca Stefoff

CHELSEA HOUSE PUBLISHERS
Philadelphia

Chelsea House Publishers

Contributing Author: Jane Manaster

Copyright © 1999 by Chelsea House Publishers,
a division of Main Line Book Co.
All rights reserved.
Printed and bound in the United States of America.

First Printing

1 3 5 7 9 8 6 4 2

Library of Congress Cataloging-in-Publication Data

Stefoff, Rebecca.
West Bank / Gaza Strip.

Includes index.
Summary: Surveys the history, topography, people, and culture of the
West Bank and the Gaza Strip, with an emphasis on current economy,
industry, and place in the political world.
1. West Bank—Juvenile literature. 2. Gaza Strip—Juvenile literature.
[1. West Bank. 2. Gaza Strip]
I. Title
DS110.W47J36   1988   956.95′3   87-18243

ISBN 0-7910-4771-7

◄ C O N T E N T S ►

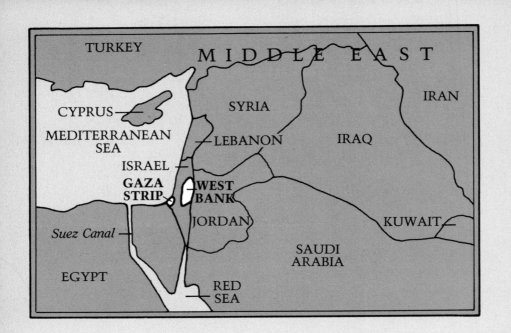

MEDITERRANEAN SEA

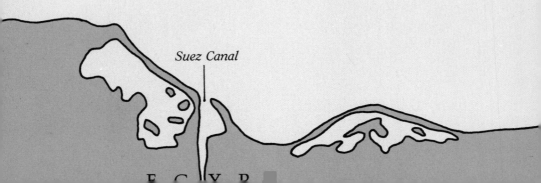

Suez Canal

◄ FACTS AT A GLANCE ►

Land and People

Total Area	2,410 square miles (6,263 square kilometers)
Total Population	2.6 million

West Bank

Area	2,270 square miles (5,900 sq km)
Population	1.66 million
Population Density	730 people per square mile (280 per sq km)
Major Cities	Jericho, Bethlehem, Hebron
Ethnic Groups	Palestinian Arabs, 98 percent; Israeli Jews, 2 percent

Gaza Strip

Area	140 square miles (363 sq km)
Population	929,000
Population Density	6,635 people per square mile (2,560 per sq km)
Major City	Gaza
Ethnic Groups	Almost entirely Palestinian Arab except for a small number of Israeli Jews

Economy

West Bank

Industry   Agriculture, tiles and ceramics, leather working, and handicrafts (including mother-of-pearl items and embroidery)

Currency   New Israeli shekel

Employment Statistics   Construction, 28%; agriculture, 22%; small-company industry, 15%; a varying number of people work in Israel

Gaza Strip

Industry   Citrus and vegetable farming, textiles, handicrafts

Currency   New Israeli shekel

Employment Statistics   Construction, 33%; agriculture, 20%; commerce, restaurants, and hotels, 15%; small-company industry, 10%; a varying number of people work in Israel

Government

The government of both territories is in a transitional state as Israeli administration is transferred to the Palestinian Authority. The first phase of the transition began in 1994.

◄HISTORY AT A GLANCE►

by 8000 B.C.	Small family groups of hunter-gatherers have settled in permanent communities in Palestine. One early settlement is Jericho, perhaps the world's oldest city.
by 3000 B.C.	The people of Palestine are creating pottery, weaving cloth, and forging bronze tools. The land is called Canaan and the people are called Canaanites.
1700 B.C.	The Hyksos people invade Canaan from the east. They conquer Canaan and Egypt. Many Hyksos, including the ancestors of the Hebrew people, settle in Canaan.
about 1600 B.C.	Egypt drives out the Hyksos rulers and takes control of Canaan.
about 1300 B.C.	Egyptian control of Canaan weakens and the Canaanites recover their independence.
1100s B.C.	The Philistines invade from the west and three new groups of Hebrews invade from the east. At the same time, a Hebrew tribe called the Israelites returns to Canaan from Egypt. Together, the Hebrews defeat the Canaanites. The Philistines establish many settlements on the coast. Gaza is one of their greatest cities.
1020 B.C.	King Saul unites the Israelite tribes into a single kingdom.
900s B.C.	Kings David and Solomon raise Israel to the peak of its power and wealth.

800s B.C.	Israel becomes two separate kingdoms, called Judah and Israel.
700s to 300s B.C.	The Syrian, Babylonian, and Persian empires control the region.
300s to about 1 B.C.	Palestine belongs to Alexander the Great, then to Egyptian and Turkish-Syrian empires. Hebrew leaders resist their conquerors and hope to reestablish an independent Hebrew kingdom.
63 B.C.	Pompey the Great captures Palestine for Rome. The Hebrews, now called Jews, revolt against Roman rule but are unsuccessful.
A.D. 70	Jerusalem becomes the headquarters of a Roman legion.
100s	The Romans coin the name Palestine for the region south of Syria.
132	A Jewish revolt against Roman rule is crushed. Most surviving Jews flee to other parts of the Mediterranean world. Jewish power in Palestine comes to an end.
300s to 600s	Palestine belongs to the Western Roman Empire and later to the Byzantine (Eastern Roman) Empire. The population increases, and Christianity becomes the major religion of the region.
638 to 640	Muslim warriors from Arabia conquer Palestine and Syria. Palestine becomes a center of Arab culture and commerce. The population gradually becomes mostly Arab and Muslim.
1095	The First Crusade recaptures Palestine from the Arabs.
1099	The Crusaders capture Jerusalem and set up a Christian state called the kingdom of Jerusalem that includes the West Bank and the Gaza Strip.

by 1291	The last Crusaders are driven out of Palestine by Muslim Arabs.
1300s and 1400s	Palestine suffers through a century of drought, plague, neglect, and economic stagnation.
1516	The Ottoman Empire, a Muslim power based in Turkey, conquers Palestine. Ottoman rule continues for four centuries.
1801	Napoleon Bonaparte captures Gaza with a French army but his army is turned back by British and Ottoman forces.
1831 to 1840	Muhammad Ali, the Ottoman governor of Egypt, rules Palestine with his son. He permits freedom of travel and the practice of Christianity. The population remains mostly Arab and Muslim.
1840	The Ottomans resume direct control of Palestine. Great Britain, France, and other nations set up trading centers in Jerusalem, Gaza, and other cities.
late 1800s	Jewish settlers from Germany, France, and Russia establish colonies in underpopulated parts of Palestine.
1917 to 1918	Britain defeats Turkish forces allied with Germany in World War I and captures Palestine. Turkey's Ottoman Empire is dismantled after the war.
1919	The League of Nations gives Great Britain temporary responsibility for governing Palestine. Thousands of Jewish immigrants arrive, and resentment and violence begin to brew between the Jews and the Arabs because both groups regard Palestine as their rightful homeland.
1947	The United Nations announces a plan to divide Palestine between the Jews and the Arabs. The

Jews approve of the plan; the Arabs reject it. Both groups prepare for battle.

1948   Great Britain formally withdraws from the administration of Palestine. Jewish leaders immediately announce the founding of the nation of Israel. Surrounding Arab nations invade Israel, but by the end of the year the Israelis hold much of Palestine. Egypt takes control of the Gaza Strip and Jordan annexes the West Bank region of Palestine.

1956   Israel attacks Egypt and captures the Gaza Strip, but returns it to Egyptian control in 1957.

1967   During the Six-Day War, Israel captures the West Bank, the Gaza Strip, and other Arab territory.

1969   Yasir Arafat becomes chairman of the Palestine Liberation Organization (PLO). The PLO uses both politics and terrorism to try to return Palestine to Arab control.

1973   Egypt and Syria attack Israel. A peace settlement is negotiated, but the Gaza Strip and the West Bank remain under Israeli control.

1974   Arafat speaks to the United Nations, urging the world to recognize the rights of the homeless Palestinians.

1982   Israel attacks Lebanon, hoping to destroy PLO bases in the country. Several Israeli military leaders are accused of allowing Lebanese Christian soldiers to massacre Palestinian refugees in two refugee camps in Beirut.

1988   Arafat tells the United Nations that the PLO will recognize Israel as a sovereign state. Jordan gives up administrative responsibility for the West Bank. The West Bank and Gaza Strip are administered by an Israeli military government.

1991   At the Madrid Conference convened by the United States and Soviet Union to promote peace negotiations, Israelis and Arabs have their first-ever direct policy talks.

1993   Israel and PLO sign declaration of principles on self-government for Palestinians.

1994   Dozens of Palestinians are killed or wounded when an Israeli settler opens fire on worshipers at a mosque in Hebron. Nevertheless, some government responsibilities are transferred to Palestinians. PLO chairman Arafat, Israeli prime minister Yitzhak Rabin, and Israeli foreign minister Shimon Peres receive the Nobel Peace Prize.

1995   Despite the assassination of Rabin, the peace agreement stays on track, and the PLO takes over further administrative responsibility.

1996   Arafat is elected president of the Palestinian Council, a legislative body that represents the Palestinian people. Palestinian and Israeli authorities cooperate in planning an industrial zone in Gaza.

late 1990s   Political stalling and terrorist attacks continue to threaten the peace process.

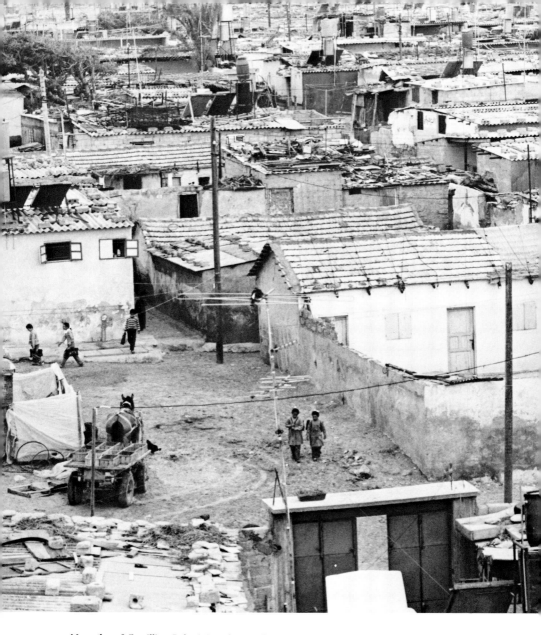

More than 2.5 million Palestinians live in the West Bank and Gaza Strip. About half of them continue to live in refugee camps such as this one in the Gaza Strip.

The Palestinians and the World

The West Bank and the Gaza Strip are two small, densely populated territories located on the borders of the nation of Israel. Most of their inhabitants are Palestinian Arabs. For almost 30 years, Israel governed both territories. Now, the West Bank and Gaza Strip are moving toward self-rule, but the transition is difficult.

Many Israelis do not want to give up the territories. Many Palestinians are impatient for the Israelis to be gone. For decades, the West Bank and Gaza Strip have been a source of conflict between Israel on one side and the Palestinians and their Arab supporters on the other. Violence has erupted frequently.

This conflict, which has helped make the Middle East one of the most troubled regions in the world today, has its roots in the long and complicated history of the region. The West Bank and the Gaza Strip, along with Israel and parts of Egypt, Syria, and Jordan, were once part of a country called Palestine. The name Palestine comes from the Philistines, a seafaring people who settled on the Mediterranean coast of the country in the 12th century B.C. Gaza, now located in the Gaza Strip, was one of the important cities of the Philistine kingdom. The region once called Palestine also includes one of the world's earliest settled regions. On the West Bank, the city of Jericho is believed to be the world's oldest city; it has been inhabited for about 10,000 years.

Palestine was conquered by almost every great empire or nation that rose to power in the Mediterranean and Middle Eastern worlds. Between the 23d century B.C. and the 20th century A.D., the region suffered invasion and occupation by Egypt (several times), Assyria, Persia, Macedonia, Rome, Byzantium, Arabia, and Turkey. Moreover, Palestine was the site of many of the most important events in three religions: Judaism, Christianity and Islam.

While the Philistines were colonizing the coast in the 12th century B.C., a tribe called the Hebrews (the ancestors of today's Jews)

In the 7th century, an Arab army led by the Caliph Omar captured Jerusalem and made Palestine part of the Arab Empire.

settled in the hilly region near the Sea of Galilee and the Dead Sea. The Hebrews were united by their religion, which was different from all the other religions of the ancient Western world because the Hebrews believed in only one god. The Hebrews believed that God had led them to Palestine and had promised it to them as their homeland; they called Palestine the Promised Land.

But the Hebrews, who eventually formed two kingdoms, Judah and Israel, were surrounded by stronger powers and were unable to defeat them. In the 1st century B.C., the Romans conquered the region. The Romans were harsh rulers who persecuted the Hebrews (now called Jews). Many Jews were killed in revolts against Roman

rule, and the Romans reacted by gradually forcing most of the Jews of Palestine to leave.

In the 7th century, the religion of Islam arose in Arabia and swept through the Middle East, North Africa, and central Asia, uniting the wandering Arabian tribes into a strong fighting kingdom. By 641, Palestine had fallen to Arab conquerors, and Arab Muslims (followers of Islam) began to settle in the region. Except for a few brief periods of Christian rule during the Crusades, it remained in Muslim hands until the 20th century.

During World War I, Palestine was controlled by the Turkish Ottoman Empire, which fought with Germany and Austria-Hungary against the United States and the British, French, and other European powers. When Germany was defeated at the end of the war, the victors broke up the Ottoman Empire. In 1919, the League of Nations, the forerunner of the United Nations, assigned Great Britain to govern Palestine until it could achieve independence.

At this time, the foundations were laid for the conflict that continues today between Arabs and Jews. Since the late 19th century, Jews living in Eastern Europe and Russia had been migrating to Palestine and forming their own communities. The Jewish migration was sparked by Zionism, a movement that called for the Jewish resettlement of Palestine. The Zionist movement grew out of the long-held desire of the Jewish people, who were scattered throughout the countries of the world and often persecuted, to have a homeland of their own in Palestine.

The Arabs living in Palestine resented the Jewish immigration because they had lived in Palestine for many centuries and considered it their home. The Jews, however, believed that Palestine was their home because they had lived there in ancient times and had been driven out. Great Britain allowed the Jews to settle in Palestine, where they built villages and farms. Afraid of being outnumbered by the Jews, the Palestinian Arabs asked Britain to grant Palestine its independence and to stop the Jewish immigration. When the British tried to do so, Jews around the world protested.

As increasing numbers of European Jews fleeing persecution settled in Palestine, tension between the Jews and the Arabs intensified and often erupted into acts of violence and terrorism. At the end of World War II, Great Britain announced that it would no longer be responsible for governing Palestine and turned the problem over to the United Nations, which voted in 1947 to partition (split) Palestine into Palestinian and Jewish states.

The Jewish people declared on May 14, 1948, that their land was the independent state of Israel. Thousands of Palestinians, not wanting to live under Jewish rule, fled to the Palestinian part of the region and to neighboring Arab countries. Arab armies came to the aid of the Palestinians and invaded Israel, but they were defeated.

Israel and the Arab states of Syria, Egypt, and Jordan have been at war many times since the 1948 war. The most important wars since then have been the Suez War in 1956, the Six-Day War in 1967, the October (or Yom Kippur) War in 1973, and the war in Lebanon in 1982.

After the 1948 war, Jordan seized the West Bank, which makes up most of the original Arab state of Palestine as defined by the United Nations. Meanwhile, Egypt took control of the Gaza Strip. Then, in the 1967 war, Israel occupied both territories, and from then on they were held by Israel but not incorporated into the Israeli state. Finally, as a result of negotiations between Arabs and Israelis in the early 1990s, the territories began to tread a path toward self-rule.

Over the years, several Palestinian groups have declared that they wanted the Israelis driven out of all of Palestine. This sentiment weakened when Yasir Arafat, the head of the Palestine Liberation Organization (PLO), recognized the existence of Israel as a state in 1988. While there is still no overall agreement about the future relationship between Israel and the occupied territories, violence and warfare are no

Israeli soldiers search the body of a Jordanian soldier killed during an Israeli raid on Jordan.

longer favored officially by either side. Many of the Palestinian Arabs in the West Bank and Gaza are refugees who do not have a country and have never been welcomed by neighboring Arab states. They look forward to an independent Palestinian state existing alongside Israel.

Still, however, there are radicals on both sides who refuse to accept the peace process. In 1987, militant Palestinians launched a campaign of often-violent strikes and demonstrations known as the *intifada*, vowing to get rid of Israel and the Israelis. Support for the *intifada* (literally, "uprising") was never absolute among Palestinians, and since then the extremists have declined in popularity. But the threat of violence from certain Palestinian groups remains.

At the same time, some Israelis still believe that the West Bank and the Gaza Strip should be annexed (officially made part of Israel), and the most militant insist that the land rightfully belongs to the Jews. In 1994 an Israeli settler opened fire on Palestinian worshipers, and in 1995 Israel's prime minister was assassinated by a Jewish militant. As on the Palestinian side, the extremists are in the minority. But many middle-of-the-road Israelis continue to worry that an independent Palestinian state would allow Palestinian groups, and even certain neighboring Arab countries, to use the territory as bases for attacks on Israel.

The complexity of the problem—and the potential for violence from both sides—has been aggravated by Israeli settlements in the West Bank. In 1990, after the fall of Communism in the Soviet bloc, some 350,000 Jewish immigrants arrived in Israel from the former Soviet Union and Eastern Europe. Hundreds of thousands more followed over the next few years. One result of this population increase was an immediate need for more housing. This led to additional settlements, especially in the West Bank, on land that the Palestinians considered to be theirs. Israelis have continued to move into new housing developments and farm communities in the occupied territories. These settlements have prompted many Palestinians to believe that Israel will never give up control of the land.

A dispute unresolved for so many years is not likely to disappear soon. The peace process has been subject to many starts and stops, and there are some who would like to derail it entirely. Nevertheless, the slow progress toward Palestinian self-rule and peaceful coexistence offers hope for the future.

Jericho, pictured above, is the oldest continuously inhabited city in the world. Located on the edge of the Jordan Valley, it has changed little over the years.

The Land

Only about 25 miles (40 kilometers) apart at their closest points, the West Bank and the Gaza Strip are similar in many ways. Both contain fertile areas that have been farmed for thousands of years, and both support almost identical native plant and animal life. However, their size and geographical features are very different.

The West Bank is more than 16 times larger than the Gaza Strip, and has a varied terrain that ranges from the hot, dry Jordan River Valley to the fertile, rugged Judaean and Samarian hills. Irrigation has made almost every part of the region productive, but the uplands are particularly rich, supporting pastures, farms, and even small forests. The smaller Gaza Strip is uniformly flat and contains no rivers, but its entire western coast faces the Mediterranean Sea.

The West Bank

The West Bank covers an area of 2,270 square miles (5,900 square kilometers) between Israel and Jordan. It is roughly 87 miles (140 kilometers) long from north to south and about 30 miles (50 km) wide from east to west. The city of Jerusalem, which is included in the state of Israel, cuts sharply into the territory's western border. The West Bank received its name when Jordan occupied the land in

1949; the addition of new territory meant that Jordan was divided into a West Bank and an East Bank region separated by the Jordan river. The Jordan River Valley and the Judaean Hills to the west are the two main features of the West Bank's terrain.

Sometimes called the Jordan Trench, the Jordan River Valley is a deep rift in the earth's surface. It is part of a great system of rifts that runs from southeast Africa to the Middle East. The width of the Jordan River Valley varies from 1.5 to 14 miles (2.5 to 23 kilometers). At the center of the valley is the Dead Sea, which is the lowest point on the earth's land surface — 1,315 feet (398 meters) below sea level.

The Jordan River drains the waters of the Sea of Galilee and many smaller rivers and streams into the Dead Sea, which has no outlet. The Dead Sea is about 48 miles (75 kilometers) long and 9 miles (15 km) wide. It's eastern shore belongs to Jordan; the northern half of its western shore belongs to the West Bank and the southern half belongs to Israel.

The Dead Sea received its name because its warm water contains more salt than any other body of water in the world; no fish, animals, or plants can live in it. Its only inhabitants are tiny, invisible, single-celled organisms that can tolerate the high salt level. Because objects float easily in salty water, even people who do not know how to swim can float in the Dead Sea — it is almost impossible to stay underwater. However, the Dead Sea is not a pleasant place to swim because the water causes eyes to sting and skin to itch.

The salty waters of the Dead Sea may make swimming unpleasant, but people flock to the surrounding health resorts in order to bathe in rocky pools fed by hot springs of mineral water. Some visitors believe that the warm mud near these springs can cure arthritis and other diseases. A few of these hot springs have been used as spas for thousands of years; according to legend, King David of the Bible used to bathe in the springs after battles. During the first part of the 20th century, the Dead Sea resort at Lido, in the West

Bank, was famous. It has been closed since the Israeli occupation, but other resorts on the Dead Sea's Israeli shore still serve Jews and Arabs, as well as tourists from all over the world.

The Jordan River Valley is not a desert, but it is quite hot and dry. Jericho, one of the major cities on the West Bank, sits on the side of the valley. Temperatures range from 61° Fahrenheit (16° Centigrade) in the winter to more than 90° F (32° C) in the summer. Some places in the valley have recorded summertime temperatures as high as 131° F (54° C). The valley receives only about 8 inches (203 millimeters) of rain each year.

In the northern part of the West Bank, along the Jordan River, an elaborate irrigation system draws water from the river for farms and orchards. Some villages still rely on ancient, crumbling irriga-

The Jordan River cuts its path through the hot, dry Jordan River Valley.

tion canals that use wooden water pumps powered by donkeys or cattle. But many of the irrigation sites—especially those built by the Israelis since their 1967 occupation of the West Bank—have modern, diesel-engine pumps, sprinklers, and miles of metal pipes. Since recorded history began, irrigation has made this part of the Jordan River Valley fertile and productive.

The Dead Sea's southern shores are salty marshes where little vegetation can grow. Even in this inhospitable terrain, however, a few oases (areas where underground springs can be tapped for water wells to support communities) flourish. In addition, Israeli workers have built several large irrigation and fertilization projects that may make this marsh area productive in the future.

The other main feature of the West Bank's terrain is the Galilean-Samarian-Judaean Highlands, an area of hills and plateaus that rises to the west of the valley. This area is traditionally divided into two regions: Samaria, located to the north of Jerusalem, and Judaea, south of Jerusalem. The hills run from north to south and reach heights of between 2,300 and 3,000 feet (700 and 900 meters).

The Samarian Hills contain the peaks of Carmel, Gilboa, Ebal, Shiloh, and Gerizim. Between the peaks lie broad, flat basins, or valleys, the largest of which are Dothan and Nablus. The valleys are threaded with small streams; those in the eastern part of Samaria flow down into the Jordan River, and those in the west flow into the Mediterranean Sea.

The Samarian Hills receive about 27 inches (686 millimeters) of rain each year, making this one of the best-watered parts of the West Bank. Much of the land is used as pasture for sheep. Melons, cereal grains, and olives grow in Samaria without irrigation, along with some small forests of cedar, oak, and cypress trees.

The Judaean Hills, south of Jerusalem, are much more rugged than the Samarian Hills. Their barren, rocky peaks and a high limestone plateau are separated from the Mediterranean coastal plain by

The Gaza Strip is a flat, fertile land dotted with farms and orchards.

the Shepelah, a 5- to 8-mile- (8- to 13-kilometer-) wide belt of soft, chalky limestone hills. The Shepelah forms the southwestern boundary of the West Bank.

Judaea is drier than Samaria. Rainfall averages about 10 inches (254 millimeters) a year near Jerusalem and only 4 inches (102 mm) in the far south. There are a few patches of cultivated farmland, mostly near the city of Hebron (called al-Khalil by the Palestinians), but much of the region can support only small, scattered flocks of sheep.

Plant and animal life in the West Bank includes many species adapted to semidesert conditions. In addition to the cedar, oak, and cypress trees of the Samaria region, some pines and palms grow in the Jordan River Valley. Many kinds of grass cover the highlands, which also support bushes such as the sagebrush.

Most of the native animals are small: rabbits, jackals, foxes, wildcats, mole rats, and mongoose. Wolves, hyenas, gazelles, and wild boars used to live throughout the highlands, but these species became rare as the human population increased. Centipedes, snakes, scorpions, and lizards are common. Native birds include the golden eagle, the vulture, the pigeon, and the partridge.

The Gaza Strip

The Gaza Strip is much smaller than the West Bank. Bordering Israel, Egypt, and the Mediterranean Sea, it covers an area of 140 square miles (363 square kilometers), about 25 miles (40 kilometers) in length and 8 miles (13 km) wide at its widest point. Its entire western border faces the Mediterranean Sea.

The Gaza Strip is a fertile region. It is the southwestern corner of a broad, flat plain called the Plain of Philistia, after the ancient kingdom of the Philistines. Since prehistoric times, the Plain of Philistia has supported many flourishing farms and orchards. The Gaza Strip today continues to be intensively cultivated, with about three-fourths of the land used for agriculture. The southwestern part of the strip, approaching the border with Egypt, is somewhat sandier and less fertile.

Flat, level, and unbroken by any rivers or mountains, the Gaza Strip lacks spectacular scenery or noteworthy geographical features. Its climate is Mediterranean, which means that the Gaza Strip receives most of its 10 inches (254 millimeters) of rain during the winter months and is seldom cold. Temperatures are about the same as those of the West Bank, except during winter, when breezes blowing inland from the sea make the Gaza Strip a few degrees cooler than the Jordan River Valley.

The native plant and animal life of the Gaza Strip is no different from that of the West Bank, except for the presence of dolphins and saltwater fish in the coastal waters. However, because the Gaza Strip has been densely populated and farmed for many hundreds of years, wildlife is rarer here than in the hilly regions of the West Bank.

Archaeological Treasures

The West Bank and the Gaza Strip contain many relics of mankind's past. Archaeologists have been busy in these two territories and in Israel ever since archaeology began in the 19th century. The cities,

In 1947 a Bedouin boy discovered the Dead Sea scrolls in a West Bank cave.

tombs, and fragments of pottery they have found tell the story of life in the region before written history.

One of the most important archaeological sites in the West Bank is Jericho, which is generally believed to be the oldest city in the world. Scientists estimate that as early as 7500 B.C. it housed a community of between 2,000 and 3,000 people. Stone walls encircled the settlement's mud-brick houses, and a system of irrigation ditches were used to water its fields. The earliest inhabitants also built a great stone tower, and although the city was torn down and rebuilt several times over the centuries, the bottom 30 feet (9 meters) of the tower still stands. The city's remarkable walls probably gave rise to the biblical legend of the walls of Jericho.

In 1947, an Arab boy made one of the most astonishing archae-ological discoveries of modern times. While herding goats on a hill-side at Khirbat Qumran (Ruins of Qumran), south of Jericho near the Dead Sea coast, he threw a pebble into a small cave and heard pottery shatter. When he looked into the cave, he found dozens of ancient manuscripts that had been rolled up and placed in clay jars, where they had lain forgotten for centuries.

Scientists investigated the boy's discovery and eventually found hundreds of manuscripts in 11 caves. Known as the Dead Sea scrolls, these manuscripts tell many of the same stories found in the Old Tes-tament of the Bible. The scrolls, which had belonged to a small Jew-ish community that was massacred by the Romans in A.D. 68, had lain hidden for almost 19 centuries, protected by the jars and preserved by the dry climate. Scholars are still studying the information these scrolls hold about the region's early history.

The Gaza Strip has two archaeological sites of special interest. One is Tell el-Fara, near Gaza. In the 1930s, scientists uncovered evi-dence of ancient houses dug into the earth like artificial caves and in-habited in about 4000 B.C. The inhabitants used copper axes and cre-ated carved ivory ornaments. Most were probably herdsmen who roamed the plains with their flocks. Archaeologists hope to find more traces of Tell el-Fara's history.

The other major discovery in the Gaza Strip occurred in 1968. An Israeli husband-and-wife archaeological team noticed that the an-tiquities markets of Jerusalem had suddenly become flooded with Egyptian-style jewelry and pottery from the 13th century B.C. These relics bore traces of yellow sand like that found on the Gaza coast. The archaeologists decided that tomb robbers had unearthed a tomb somewhere near Gaza.

After some detective work, they located the tomb site in a plowed field among sand dunes not far from the sea, south of the village of Deir el-Balah. Archaeologists began to dig at the site and were amazed to discover first a large cemetery and later the remains of a massive military fortress. The archaeologists believe that Deir el-Balah was an Egyptian colony built during the reign of Seti I, who ruled Egypt from about 1318 to 1304 B.C. The Egyptians apparently conquered the region and built the fortress to maintain control of the seacoast. As long as 3,000 years ago, the Gaza Strip had already become a scene of conflict between Egypt and the land that would one day become Israel.

A small seated figure, probably a priest, dates from Lagash, around 2400 B.C.

Early History

The earliest inhabitants of the West Bank and the Gaza Strip were wandering tribes of hunter-gatherers (people who did not practice farming or herding but lived by killing wild game and gathering edible plants). These people made tools such as axes, spears, and sickles out of flint, bone, and ivory. At first they lived in caves, but later they learned to build simple huts or tents from branches and skins. About 10,000 years ago, small family groups began to settle in permanent communities, creating the region's first towns.

By about 3000 B.C., the people living in the region had mastered the arts of building in stone, creating pottery, weaving cloth, and forging tools and weapons from bronze. The development of this last skill marked the beginning of the Bronze Age. During the Bronze Age, the population grew until almost all the land was inhabited. The population was evenly divided between nomadic (wandering) herdsmen in the hill country and town-dwellers and farmers in the plains and along the coast. Although they belonged to many different tribes, these early inhabitants were called Canaanites, and the West Bank, Gaza, and Israel were called Canaan.

In about 1700 B.C., a powerful Asiatic people called the Hyksos came from the east of Canaan and conquered both the Canaanites and the neighboring Egyptians. The Hyksos invaders included a large group of Semitic (southwest Asian) people called the Habiru, who settled among the Canaanites. The word "Hebrew," the biblical name for the early Jews and their language, may have come from Habiru.

After about a century, the Egyptians drove out the Hyksos and ruled Canaan until about 1300 B.C. The Canaanite princes paid yearly tributes (taxes of silver, gold, sheep, or grain) to the pharaohs (rulers) of Egypt, but these distant Egyptian overlords had little influence on life in Canaan. Egyptian rule weakened, and the Canaanites began to recover their independence. In the 12th century B.C., however, two new waves of invaders assaulted them from the west and from the east.

From the west came the seafaring Philistines, whose original home was the islands of the Aegean Sea near Greece. They occupied most of the southern coast of what is now Israel and established many coastal settlements. Gaza, the major city of today's Gaza Strip, was one of the largest Philistine cities.

At the same time, three new Hebrew tribes entered Canaan from the east: the Edomites, the Moabites, and the Ammonites. Each of these tribes consisted of families clustered into scattered clans. The

Moses' descent from Mount Sinai with the Ten Commandments is one of the many Old Testament stories that took place in early Palestine.

Hebrews were nomadic herdsmen who lived in tents and followed their flocks of sheep and goats from pasture to pasture. They practiced a monotheistic religious faith, meaning that they believed in only one god. This set them apart from neighboring peoples, all of whom worshipped many gods.

During this period a fourth and much larger Hebrew tribe made its way into Canaan from Egypt. Originally a part of the Hyksos population of Canaan, these Hebrews called themselves the Israelites. Several generations earlier, a severe famine had driven them out of the hills of Canaan into Egypt. The Egyptians welcomed them at first but then enslaved them. Now greatly increased in number, they returned to Canaan under the leadership of Moses, the patriarch (senior male leader) of their clans. Many of the stories in the Old Testament of the Bible are based on events that occurred at this time.

The Israelites joined the Hebrews already living in Canaan and together they defeated the Canaanites. But this loose alliance soon broke down as the tribes began to war with one another. The leaders of the tribes realized that the Hebrews must unite if they were to defeat the Philistines, who had begun to expand their settlements from the coast. In 1020 B.C., the tribes agreed to accept the leadership of Saul, who was named their king.

Saul fought the Philistines living on the coast and died in battle in about 1000 B.C. His successor, King David, defeated the Philistines and expanded the borders of the Hebrew kingdom to include much of present-day Lebanon, Syria, Jordan, and Egypt.

David was succeeded by his son, King Solomon. This famous king made the Hebrew nation an important power in the ancient world. Israel became wealthy through mining and trade (Solomon was the first Israelite king to trade with the Arabs of the Arabian peninsula). In order to complete his many expensive building projects—including a great temple at Jerusalem and a stable for 400 horses and chariots in northern Israel—Solomon raised taxes and required many Israelites to work in labor gangs.

After his death, the northern half of the kingdom broke away. It became known as the kingdom of Israel, and the southern part was called the kingdom of Judah. Over the next several centuries, the two kingdoms alternately fought and made peace with each other and with neighboring states. This was the era of the great prophets and religious teachers Elijah and Elisha, whose words were recorded in the Old Testament.

In the middle of the 8th century B.C., the kingdom of Israel fell to the Assyrian empire, which was based in modern Syria. Judah repelled the Assyrians and continued to prosper as an independent kingdom until the Babylonian empire of Persia (now Iran) rose to power in the Middle East. In 587 B.C., the Babylonians stormed and destroyed Jerusalem, capturing many Hebrews and taking them into exile in Babylonia. Four decades later, the Hebrews were allowed to return to Judah. They began to rebuild Jerusalem and reestablished the practice of their faith, now called Judaism.

In the 4th century B.C., the armies of Alexander the Great of Macedonia (a region near the border between present-day Greece and Turkey) conquered most of the ancient Western world. Judah became part of Alexander's empire, but he was not interested in occupying the land. He wanted only to use Judah as a path to the conquest of Egypt. He left the Hebrews' religions and customs alone and made a Hebrew high priest head of state.

From the 4th through the 1st centuries B.C., Judah belonged first to the Ptolemaic empire, which was established in Egypt by Ptolemy, one of Alexander's generals, and then to the Seleucid empire of Turkey and Syria.

Little is known of life in Judah during this period. The population seems to have remained evenly divided between town-dwellers in the coastal regions and farmers and nomads in the hills. The region was not a unified country but rather a series of small city-states, such as Samaria, Judaea, and Jerusalem. Some cities issued their own coins, engraved with images of the Hebrew high priests. Judah exported large amounts of cereals, olive oil, and wine to Egypt and its rulers conducted a brisk slave trade with the Egyptians and Turks.

In 168 B.C., the Hebrews rose in revolt against their Seleucid overlords. Led by Judas Maccabaeus, they protested the introduction of Greek and Syrian idols and rites into the holy places of Judaism. Judas defeated several Seleucid generals and drove their priests out of Jerusalem before he was killed in battle in 161 B.C.

Judas Maccabaeus led the Hebrew revolt against the Seleucid Empire.

Judas's descendants continued to resist the empire. Control of Judah passed back and forth between the Hebrew kings and priests and the Seleucids for nearly a century. One strong Hebrew leader of this period was a woman, Salome Alexandra; she died in 67 B.C.

The Hebrews were weakened in their struggle against outside powers when two powerful groups arose within the priesthood. One group, the Pharisees, insisted that the Hebrews should closely follow their ancient traditions. The other group, the Sadducees, believed that some elements of Greek and Persian culture should be allowed to mingle with Hebrew culture. The rivalry between these two groups threatened to tear Hebrew society apart.

Seleucid power waned in the middle years of the 1st century B.C., and it appeared that the Hebrew people might be able to re-establish their own independent kingdom. However, a new imperial power—Rome—appeared on the scene to scoop up the pieces of the Seleucid empire.

In 63 B.C., the Roman leader Pompey the Great conquered the Seleucids and seized control of their lands, including Palestine. He appointed one of Judas's descendants high priest, but refused to give him the title of king. Pompey also made the Hebrews pay taxes to Rome and put some Hebrew cities under the control of the Roman governor of Syria.

When Pompey died, the Roman emperor Julius Caesar gave Roman citizenship to Antipater, one of the descendants of Judas Maccabaeus. In return for accepting Roman rule, Antipater received the title "procurator (military governor) of Judaea" (Judaea was the Roman name for the ancient kingdoms of Israel and Judah). Antipater's son Herod and Herod's descendants governed Judaea for the Romans until A.D. 6. After this, Romans filled the post; one of them, Pontius Pilate, was procurator when Jesus Christ was crucified.

The Romans were brutal rulers, and the Hebrews, now called Jews, revolted against them in a series of bitter military campaigns.

In 67, the Roman general Vespasian (later an emperor) arrived in Judaea with 60,000 soldiers and crushed the rebellion. In 70, the Romans destroyed much of Jerusalem, and a Roman legion set up headquarters in the city. Roman control over the area was now complete, and the Romans built a new city called Neapolis on the site of modern-day Nablus in the West Bank.

During the 2d century, the Romans named their province of Judaea, which was located south of Syria, "Syria Palaestina"—the Latin form of Philistia. From this time on, the region was known as Palestine.

In 132, the Roman emperor Hadrian decided to build a new Roman city on the site of old Jerusalem. Angered, the Jews united in a fierce rebellion. The Romans put down the revolt with great force, destroying nearly 1,000 villages throughout Palestine and killing more than 500,000 people. Most of the surviving Jews fled to North Africa, Spain, and other remote areas. Those who remained settled in Galilee, in the northern part of the province. Jewish power in Palestine came to an end.

During one of many disorders, British troops, like these machine gunners in
Jaffa, battled Arab marauders.

Many Claims to One Land

Successive empires ruled Palestine during the next 1,700 years, changing the political and cultural landscape of the region. After the 2d century, few Jews remained in Palestine, and neighboring Syrian and Semitic peoples flowed into the region. The Romans founded new cities, and grain from Palestinian fields helped feed the Roman Empire. When the Roman Empire split into the Eastern (Byzantine) and the Western Roman empires, Palestine fell under the control of the Byzantine Empire, based in Turkey. After the 4th century, the Byzantine Empire's leaders converted to Christianity. They permitted Christian pilgrims, monks, and hermits from all parts of the empire to flock to Palestine to visit and worship at the places where Jesus Christ had lived, taught, and died. Churches, chapels, and monasteries arose throughout the land.

In 352, the small Jewish population of Galilee revolted unsuccessfully against the Byzantines' oppressive rule. But for the most part, Christian Palestine was predominantly peaceful and prosperous until the early 7th century, when the Persians invaded. In 628, the Byzantines drove the Persians out and regained control of Palestine. Ten years later, however, a powerful force of Arabs marched on Palestine from the south. Driven by their belief in Islam, they defeated the Byzantines and began centuries of Islamic rule in Palestine.

The Arabs traced their ancestry to the nomadic tribes of the Arabian peninsula. By the early 7th century, many of them had embraced the religion of Islam and had become Muslims. Islam means "submission to Allah (the Muslim name for God)." The religion is based on the Koran, the holy book that contains Allah's messages to Muhammad, the founder of Islam. Religion governs all aspects of the life of a Muslim. It even includes rules on how society should be governed. Muhammad and his followers developed a political system based on Islam and imposed it and their religious views on peoples living in Arabia.

In 632, Muhammad died. His successor, Abu Bakr, who was called the caliph, began the first of many jihads (holy wars) against neighboring empires. It was Abu Bakr who sent nearly 10,000 troops into the land the Arabs called "Filastin" (Palestine), but it was only under his successor, the Caliph Omar, that the Arab army defeated the Byzantines and captured Jerusalem in 641.

Palestine's landscape changed as Islam became the predominant religion.

Palestine quickly became an important center of Arab culture. Muslims regarded Jerusalem as one of the holiest cities of Islam, because they believed the prophet Muhammad had visited the city just before he ascended into heaven. After the conquest, the Arabs built many mosques (temples or holy buildings), some of them on the sites of earlier churches or temples belonging to other faiths. Large numbers of Muslim Arabs settled in Palestine and forced the non-Muslim population to pay high taxes. Some Jews and Christians converted to Islam to avoid harsh treatment at the hands of the Muslim rulers. The population, which had been mostly Syrian and Christian, gradually became mostly Arab and Muslim.

At its peak, the Arab empire included most of North Africa, part of Spain, and all of the Middle East. Palestine was one of the nine provinces of the empire, governed by a local ruler called an *emir*. Gaza and Jerusalem were the province's chief cities.

Various Arab dynasties (family groups) fought among them-selves for control of the empire, and four powerful dynasties—the Umayyads, the Abbasids, the Ikhshidids, and the Fatimids—ruled Palestine in turn. After the Fatimid dynasty seized power in the 10th century, however, the Arabs faced the threat of a new enemy: the armies of the Christian Crusaders.

The Crusades

In 1095, Christian Western European countries sent into Palestine a huge army led by kings, princes, and bishops. Their mission, now called the First Crusade, was to win the Christian Holy Land back from the Muslims, whom they considered infidels (religious enemies).

In 1099, the Crusaders captured Jerusalem and set up a Chris-tian state called the kingdom of Jerusalem. Much larger than present-day Israel, the Crusader state included all of the West Bank and the Gaza Strip. The Crusaders built many splendid churches and cathedrals in the two territories.

The kingdom of Jerusalem was short-lived. Less than a century after its establishment, the famous Syrian warrior Saladin recaptured Palestine for the Muslims. For several centuries, Europe tried to regain control of the Holy Land, sending a series of Crusades to fight the Muslims. But none of the other Crusades was as successful as the first. The Christians held Jerusalem, Nazareth, and Bethlehem for a few years during the 13th century, but the last Crusaders were driven out of Palestine in 1291.

The 14th and 15th centuries were Palestine's Dark Ages. Almost forgotten by the Western world and neglected by its Muslim rulers, the region suffered from droughts, epidemics, and the same Black Plague that killed one-fourth of the population of Europe between 1348 and 1349. The Egyptian-based Mamluk dynasty, which had inherited the ancient Arabian Empire, did little to improve Palestine's economy during this period. Finally, in 1516, the Mamluks fell to the Ottoman Empire, a Turkish Muslim empire that rapidly gained control over most of the Middle East and North Africa.

The Ottomans ruled Palestine for four centuries, treating it as a remote backwater of the empire and isolating it from most outside

Napoleon of France considered the capture of Gaza his greatest conquest.

influences. Few travelers were allowed to enter the region, and little is known about the life of the Palestinian people during this time.

The Ottomans temporarily lost their hold on Palestine in 1801, when Napoleon of France, after capturing Egypt, decided to conquer the region. Some historians think that Napoleon (still a general at this time and not yet an emperor) wanted to copy the career of Alexander the Great, who had conquered all of western Asia. Napoleon led his armies along the coast from Egypt and captured the Palestinian city of Gaza without difficulty.

Napoleon is said to have gloated that Gaza was his greatest prize, because it was "the guardian of Africa, the gate of Asia." But he was unable to pass through the gate to conquer Syria and India. The British helped the Ottomans defeat Napoleon in Syria, and he abandoned the Middle East and turned back to France.

Soon after Napoleon withdrew from Egypt, an Egyptian named Muhammad Ali became the Ottoman viceroy (governor) of Cairo, and he quickly carved out a small empire of his own. In 1831, he and his son conquered Palestine. They ruled the region for nine years, allowing large numbers of Western travelers to visit Palestine and Jerusalem. Muhammad Ali even permitted Christian missionaries to set up churches and schools in the region. Some Palestinian Arabs converted to Christianity, but Islam remained Palestine's predominant faith.

The Ottomans resumed control of Palestine in 1840, but they could no longer keep Palestine isolated from the world. Western nations, such as Great Britain and France, had become interested in the Middle East and had begun to set up embassies and trading centers in Jerusalem and the port cities, including Gaza. In the second half of the 19th century, many Jewish immigrants from France, Germany, Eastern Europe, and Russia established colonies in the underpopulated regions of Palestine. The most important of these were the Zionist settlements.

Zionism

The Zionists believed that the Jewish people, scattered throughout the world and often persecuted, should have a national homeland; many believed that this should be established in their ancient homeland of Palestine. In 1882, a group of Russian Jews founded the first modern Jewish settlement in Palestine. They cleared land, built farms and homes, and urged other Jews to join them. Jews from many nations did so.

By 1914, the population of Palestine numbered about 690,000. Of these, 535,000 were Arab Muslims, 85,000 were Jews, and 70,000 were Arab Christians. Most of the Arabs were poor farmers or herders. About one-third of the Jews lived on some 45 Zionist farming settlements; the rest lived in small towns.

World War I brought much suffering to Palestine. Fighting between the British and the Ottoman Turks in the Middle East caused much destruction, which was made even worse by a series of epidemics and famines. At the same time, the present-day conflict between the Arabs and the Israelis began to take shape, as many of the Arab inhabitants grew resentful of the incoming Jews.

The Arabs of Palestine wanted to shake off their Ottoman overlords, and the British wanted the Arabs to fight on their side. To gain the support of the Arabs, British statesmen promised Arab leaders that Palestine would receive its independence after the war. Many Arabs then joined the British fighting forces in the Middle East. In November 1917, General Sir Edmund Allenby's British forces defeated the Turks at Gaza. In less than a year, his British and Arab troops had triumphed over the Turks in Palestine and Syria.

During the war, the Zionist movement attracted considerable international attention and sympathy. To gain Jewish support during the war years, Britain promised to promote the establishment of a national Jewish homeland in Palestine. After the war, the British government faced the difficult problem of honoring two opposing

(continued on p. 57)

SCENES OF
WEST BANK/GAZA STRIP

➤ *The Dome of the Rock mosque in Jerusalem is one of Islam's holiest sites.*

∨ *Shoppers walk through the narrow streets of the old city of Jerusalem. The eastern sector of the city was annexed by Israel after the 1967 War.*

▲ *The Israeli army laid siege to Beirut in 1982 in an attempt to crush the PLO.*

▼ *This scale model illustrates the architecture and the fortifications of ancient Jerusalem. The walls surrounding the city still stand.*

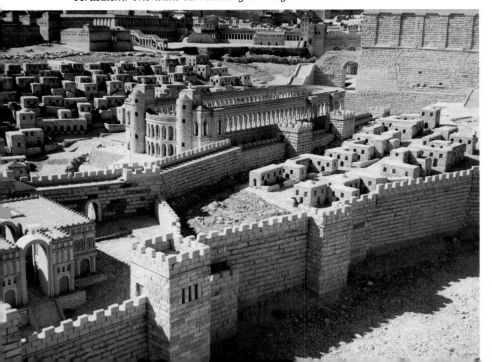

▲ *An aqueduct near the Mediterranean Sea is a reminder of Roman rule over Palestine.*

▼ *The tombs of biblical figures are found throughout the West Bank and Israel.*

▲ *Arab men in traditional headdress enjoy the afternoon as they sip strong black coffee and smoke tobacco through water pipes.*

▼ *Chunks of salt form a briny white crust on the Dead Sea. Although the Dead Sea is unusable for irrigation or for swimming, it is an important source of minerals.*

▲ *Swimmers take advantage of the cool waters of the Jordan River. The river splits the land into the West Bank and the East Bank, which is located in Jordan.*

▼ *A Palestinian woman and her child tend their farm plot as Israeli citizens demonstrate for more Israeli settlements in the West Bank.*

▲ *Arab women carry scarce firewood through the Gaza's treeless plain.*

➤ *Christian holy places abound in the former West Bank city of Jerusalem.*

⋏ *The annual Christmas procession through Bethlehem attracts thousands of Christians.*

⋎ *Bedouin Arabs barter with an Israeli trader at a camel market in Israel. The Bedouin live as nomads, carrying on a lifestyle thousands of years old.*

(continued from p. 48)

agreements. Both the Jews and the Arabs felt that Britain had promised Palestine to them. Each side tried to make Britain carry out its promises.

In 1919, the League of Nations (the forerunner of today's United Nations) entered the picture. The league gave Great Britain a mandate over Palestine, meaning that Britain was responsible for governing the territory until it could become independent. Britain tried to reassure both the Arabs and the Jews, but the two sides began to fight with each other—and both regarded the British with suspicion and dislike.

At the end of the war, floods of Jewish immigrants arrived in Palestine. Many Arabs feared that the British were going to betray them by turning the country over to the Jews. In 1920 and 1929, Palestinian Arabs rioted against the Zionists. But still more Jews wanted to enter the country. The pattern of future conflict had been set.

The relationship between the Jewish newcomers and the Arab residents worsened. The Jews wanted a place in their ancient homeland and a country of their own. But after centuries of domination by foreign powers, the Arabs were afraid of being outnumbered and overcome once again.

Jews continued to arrive in Palestine in increasing numbers, especially after the Nazis rose to power in Germany in 1935 and the murder and persecution of European Jews rose to new heights. By 1939, there were more than 200 Zionist farming settlements and some cities and towns that were entirely Jewish. The Jews in Palestine made up 30 percent of the total population.

The Arabs continued to oppose Jewish settlement. They organized an armed rebellion and a general strike that crippled Palestine in 1936. The strike ended after six months, but the revolt dragged on until 1939 and left 3,000 Arabs, 359 Jews, and 135 British dead. The British hanged more than 100 Arab revolutionaries and sent

Fighting between Arabs and Jews in the 1930s led the British to post armed guards, such as these soldiers, throughout the city of Jerusalem.

thousands to jail. It was clear that the Arabs would not peacefully share Palestine with the Jews.

Britain suggested the division of Palestine into two smaller states, one for Jews and one for Arabs. To please the Arabs, it began restricting Jewish immigration. To please the Jews, it recommended removing Arabs from the Jewish section of Palestine—by force, if necessary. But the outbreak of World War II prevented the League of Nations from discussing Britain's plan.

After the war, the independent Arab nations of the Middle East took a renewed interest in Palestine. They formed an international Arab League in 1945, and one of its goals was to make Palestine an independent Arab state. In Palestine, meanwhile, some Zionists had formed underground military groups to attack the British, hoping to drive them out of Palestine. Hostility between the Arabs and Jews continued to break out in occasional violence.

In 1947, the United Nations proposed a plan to divide Palestine into a Jewish state and an Arab state, with Jerusalem as an international district between them. Forty-five percent of the land, including the Gaza Strip and most of the West Bank, would be included in the Arab state, and 55 percent would belong to the Jewish state. The Jews agreed to the plan, but the Arabs rejected it, because it meant that many Arabs would have to choose between leaving their homes or living under Jewish rule. The British government refused to administer a plan that was not accepted by both sides and announced that it would withdraw from Palestine in May 1948.

The Jews were afraid that the United Nations would not be able to enforce the division plan; the Arabs were afraid that it would. The two groups began gathering weapons, money, and soldiers while Britain prepared to withdraw. By January 1948, more than 2,000 people had been killed in fighting between Arabs and Jews. A full-scale civil war was under way.

The Jews, with better equipment and better-trained fighters, captured several cities and defeated the Arabs in two battles. Terrorist attacks on both sides killed unarmed civilians.

Thousands of Palestinian Arabs, fearing that the Jews would seize complete control of the country when the British mandate ended, fled across the borders of Palestine. When the neighboring Arab nations of Syria, Iraq, Jordan, and Egypt saw that the Palestinian Arabs could not defeat the Jews, they agreed to send their armies into Palestine as soon as the British left. The stage was set for war.

British General Sir Edmund Allenby captured Gaza during World War I. Britain ruled all of Palestine for more than 30 years.

Moving Toward Independence

On May 14, 1948, General Sir Alan Cunningham, the last British high commissioner for Palestine, left the territory. As soon as the British flag was taken down from the front of Government House in Jerusalem, Jewish leaders proclaimed Israel an independent state that would occupy the area assigned to the Jews under the United Nations plan. The following day, May 15, tanks and troops from Syria, Jordan, Iraq, and Egypt moved into Israel.

Battles alternated with brief truces for the rest of the year. The Israeli forces proved to be stronger than the Arab forces and forced them to retreat from much of Palestine. By December, hundreds of thousands of Palestinian Arabs, fearful of the oncoming Israeli army, had abandoned their homes in cities and towns along the coast and had followed the Egyptian army as it retreated south.

When the United Nations called for a cease-fire, the refugees and most of Egypt's army were located in the area now called the Gaza Strip. Israel negotiated truces with Egypt and the other Arab countries, but did not allow the refugees to return to their homes—and many of them did not want to return to a Jewish nation. Under the terms of its agreement with Israel, Egypt took control of the Gaza Strip. Egypt, however, did not grant citizenship to the Palestinian refugees or permit them to enter Egypt. The refugees settled into crowded camps, where many of them—and their children and grandchildren—still live today.

Although Israel had established cease-fire agreements with the Arab nations, none recognized Israel's right to exist and all refused to sign a permanent peace treaty. Jordan held the area now called the West Bank and the eastern half of Jerusalem; Israel held the western half of Jerusalem. A wide no-man's-land, fenced with barbed wire, ran for 19 miles (30 kilometers) between the two sectors of the city.

By mid-1949, Israel had joined the United Nations and was recognized by many countries around the world. More than 700,000 Palestinians had fled to the Gaza Strip, the West Bank, and the Arab nations. Those living on the Jordanian-held West Bank received Jordanian citizenship, whereas refugees in the Gaza Strip or in various Arab countries became people without a country. All of them continued to insist that Palestine was theirs by right. The Arab nations remained hostile to Israel, and the Palestinians staged frequent guerrilla attacks against Israeli civilian and military targets.

In October 1956, Gamal Abdel Nasser, the president of Egypt, declared the Suez Canal to be part of Egypt. The canal, which had been built by the French, was owned by Britain and France. In retaliation for Nasser's action, the two countries sent military forces to seize the canal. Israel, which had suffered attacks from Palestinian guerrillas based in Egypt, joined with the British and the French in a secret agreement and sent its troops into the Sinai Peninsula. The United States, the Soviet Union, and the Arab nations all criticized the British-French-Israeli attack.

The United Nations halted the war in December and sent a peacekeeping force into the Sinai. France and Britain withdrew their troops. The Egyptians reopened the canal (which they had blocked with sunken ships), and the Israelis withdrew from the Gaza Strip,

Palestinian refugees flocked to camps such as this one in the Gaza Strip.

which they had captured during the war. Periodic border clashes continued between Israel, Syria, and Jordan. The third major Arab-Israeli conflict, now called the Six-Day War, began in June 1967. Egyptian President Nasser had ordered Egyptian forces to take up positions on Israel's border, and Jordan had signed a defense pact with Syria and Egypt (meaning that the three nations would help each other defend their borders.). The stage seemed set for another Arab invasion of Israeli territory.

Israel reacted to these Arab moves by striking first against Egyptian, Syrian, Jordanian, and Iraqi airfields. Egypt then declared war on Israel, and Jordan soon followed. In six days of fighting, Israeli troops captured eastern Jerusalem, the West Bank, the Gaza Strip, the Sinai Peninsula, and the Golan Heights (on the border between Israel and Syria).

Israeli military detachments and government officers moved into all of these areas, but only eastern Jerusalem officially became a part of Israel. The Israelis claimed the entire city as their national capital and moved many citizens and businesses into the former Arab section.

In November 1967, the United Nations Security Council passed Resolution 242, a document that the UN hoped would end Israeli occupation of the West Bank and Gaza Strip and, more important, lead to peace in the Middle East. Resolution 242 calls for the withdrawal of Israel's military forces from the territories occupied during the Six-Day War. It also acknowledges Israel's right to exist as a sovereign nation. Resolution 242 has played an important role in many international discussions about the future of the occupied territories. But it took almost three decades after the resolution's passage before the withdrawal of Israeli forces began.

Yasir Arafat and the PLO

Only a few years before the Six-Day War, a new element entered Middle Eastern politics. A number of Palestinian religious and student organizations united in 1964 to form the Palestine Liberation Organization (PLO), a guerrilla group dedicated to overthrowing Israel and returning Palestine to Arab hands. In 1969, Yasir Arafat became the chairman of the PLO and helped direct worldwide attention to its activities. He believed that the displaced Palestinians needed a voice in international politics, and he made the PLO into that voice—at times a loud, angry voice.

Arafat was born in 1929 in Jerusalem to a violently anti-Zionist family. He went to school first in Gaza and then in Egypt. After finishing school, he helped start a secret Arab military organization called Fatah, which carried out guerrilla warfare and acts of terrorism against the Israelis. Fatah became part of the PLO and was responsible for many of the shootings and bombings that broke the Arab-Israeli truce after 1967.

Yasir Arafat has forced the Palestinian issue into the world spotlight.

The cease-fire between Israel and the Arab nations ended on October 6, 1973, when Egypt and Syria attacked Israel. Because it began on the Jewish holy day of Yom Kippur (the Day of Atonement), this war is sometimes called the Yom Kippur War.

The Arabs fought more effectively than they had in the past, partly because their attack came as a surprise to the Israelis. Despite heavy casualties, however, the Israeli army pushed into Egypt and Syria. The war continued until November. In the spring of 1974, Israel signed new cease-fire agreements with the two Arab countries. The Arabs and the Israelis exchanged prisoners of war, and they agreed that the United Nations should station soldiers in zones between Israel, Egypt, and Syria to help keep the peace. Israel also agreed to withdraw its troops from Egypt's Sinai Peninsula over the next few years. However, it announced that it would not give up control of the Gaza Strip and the West Bank.

Two events of the following year were milestones for Arafat and the PLO. In October 1974, the leaders of all the Arab nations met in Rabat, the capital of Morocco. The Arab leaders agreed to recognize the PLO as the "sole legitimate representative of the Palestinian people." The Rabat conference, in effect, said that the Arab nations recognized Arafat as the official spokesman for the Palestinians.

In November 1974, Arafat spoke to the General Assembly of the United Nations, urging the countries of the world to recognize the plight of the homeless Palestinians. He was the first representative of a nongovernmental organization ever to address the assembly.

Arafat's political activities won some sympathy for the Arab cause, especially from the Soviet Union and other Communist countries. At the same time, however, acts of Arab guerrilla warfare and terrorism against Israelis—such as the 1972 massacre of members of the Israeli team at the Munich Olympics—angered many people around the world. PLO guerrilla groups that had formed in Palestinian refugee camps in neighboring Arab countries caused relations between the Palestinians and the Arab countries to deteriorate as well (In 1970, Jordan's King Hussein had fought a civil war with the Palestinian guerrillas in Jordan and had driven them out of the country.).

In the mid-1970s, Arafat announced that the Arabs would begin to replace violence with political persuasion to accomplish their goal of regaining Palestine. Some extremely anti-Israel Palestinian groups rejected Arafat's new strategy, and continued to practice the tactics of terrorism. These conflicts led to division in the PLO. Eventually, Arafat lost some power and prestige within the PLO and the world of international politics.

In 1977, an Arab nation stepped forward to make peace with Israel when Egyptian President Anwar Sadat flew to Jerusalem on November 19, 1977, to meet with Israeli Prime Minister Menachem Begin. Many Palestinians viewed Sadat's overture as a betrayal of their territorial claims.

After their meeting in Jerusalem, Begin and Sadat accepted United States President Jimmy Carter's invitation to hold peace talks at the President's retreat at Camp David. During the talks, Begin and Sadat agreed on several issues that had divided the two countries. Egypt agreed to recognize Israel's right to exist and agreed to establish diplomatic relations; Israel agreed to return the Sinai Peninsula to Egypt. Both agreed that these steps must also lead to a solution to Palestinian homelessness. On March 26, 1979, the two leaders signed a peace treaty in Washington, D.C.

But Egypt's peace with Israel did not end the PLO's struggle with Israel. Terrorist and guerilla attacks by the PLO continued. In June 1982, Israel decided it would try to end the PLO's ability to attack Israel by destroying Palestinian bases in Lebanon.

The Israeli army quickly moved north through Lebanon, destroying PLO sites and heavily bombing Beirut, the capital city. The Israelis laid siege to Beirut, where Arafat and most of the PLO were

U.S. President Bill Clinton brings together the late Israeli Prime Minister Yitzhak Rabin and PLO Chairman Yasir Arafat for an historic handshake after the signing of the Israeli-PLO peace accord at the White House in 1993.

located, but finally allowed an international peacekeeping force to oversee the PLO's removal from the city in August. Arafat went to Tunisia, where he set up new headquarters. Less than one month later, Christian Lebanese militia allied with Israel massacred hundreds of Palestinian refugees in the Sabra and Shatila refugee camps in Beirut.

The massacre shocked the world. An Israeli government commission investigated the incident and ruled that Israeli military officials had allowed the massacre to take place; some officers were forced to resign.

In September, 1983, Arafat returned to Lebanon where PLO forces loyal to him were fighting a bloody battle in the port city of Tripoli with several rebel PLO groups. Some of the groups were aided by the Syrian government, which wanted to topple Arafat and take control of the Palestinian resistance movement. The rebels made several attempts on Arafat's life. With the aid of Syrian tanks and troops, they surrounded Arafat's forces.

The end for Arafat seemed near, but Saudi Arabia stepped in and asked Syria to withdraw. Arafat and his men then returned to Tunisia. Despite the rebels' efforts to replace him, by 1986 tempers had cooled, and the Palestinian people as a whole continued to support Arafat as the head of the PLO.

In 1987 the Palestinian *intifada* (uprising) erupted against Israeli control. The violent campaign provoked an unexpected turn of events. Arafat addressed the United Nations in 1988 to proclaim a Palestinian state, but also to recognize the political existence of Israel. Expressing a desire for negotiated peace, he declared an end to terrorism as a tactic for independence. The move led Jordan to give up its claim to the West Bank.

In 1991, U.S. and Soviet delegates met in Madrid with Middle East representatives to promote peace talks. Palestinians, Jordanians, Syrians, and Lebanese, together with Israelis, also discussed five major issues that confronted the region: water, refugees, the environment, economic development, and security.

The greatest breakthrough came in 1993, when Arafat and Israeli prime minister Yitzhak Rabin met in Washington, D.C., to sign a Declaration of Principles on Interim Self-Government Arrangements. Though not specifying any final status for the occupied territories, this agreement detailed gradual steps toward self-government. Throughout that summer and fall, meetings were held, both secretly and publicly, to establish a Palestinian authority and to plan elections in the West Bank and Gaza Strip. The progress received global acknowledgment when Arafat, along with Rabin and Israeli foreign minister Shimon Peres, received the Nobel Prize for Peace.

Actual Israeli troop pullbacks began in 1994, at first in Jericho and Gaza, then extending to other areas. But the efforts toward peace continued to suffer numerous setbacks. In 1994 a Jewish extremist opened fire on worshipers at a mosque in Hebron, slaughtering and wounding dozens. In 1995, days after Arab suicide bombers destroyed Israeli buses in Gaza, another Israeli extremist assassinated Rabin after a peace rally. The mood in the region turned ugly, and Israeli-Palestinian talks were suspended for a time.

Meanwhile, the Popular Front for the Liberation of Palestine (PFLP) and the Democratic Front for the Liberation of Palestine (DFLP), two Palestinian groups opposed to the peace process, called for a boycott of the Palestinian elections scheduled for January 20, 1996. Their efforts failed, and Arafat was elected president of the new 88-member Palestinian Legislative Council.

By the late 1990s, while the majority of Israelis and Palestinians recognized the same goal—an independent state of Palestine at peace with neighboring Israel—each side was continuing to antagonize the other. On the one hand, the Israelis talked about withdrawing from the West Bank and Gaza, but continued to build Jewish settlements in the occupied territories. The Palestinians, despite officially condemning violence, did not succeed in stopping extremist behavior.

In spite of the stumbling blocks, Palestinian independence—which seemed little more than a dream a short time ago—has become a slowly emerging reality. More and more Palestinians and Israelis have come to realize that peace in the region is essential—and not impossible.

Most Palestinians have dark hair and dark eyes like this young girl, who is eating a lunch of pita bread and soup at her refugee camp.

The People and Their Culture

No one knows exactly how many people live in the West Bank. An accurate census has been difficult to obtain because, for many years, no single government had complete responsibility for the territory. The current best estimates of the West Bank's population place it at about 1.66 million people—more than double the population figure in the mid-1980s. That works out to about 730 people per square mile (280 per square kilometer)—slightly higher than the population density in Israel.

Figures for the population of the Gaza Strip are also based on estimates rather than on an accurate census. The most recent figures show that about 929,000 people live in the territory. With a population density of 6,635 people per square mile (2,560 per square kilometer), the Gaza Strip is one of the world's most densely populated areas.

About 83 percent of the West Bank's residents are Palestinian Arabs. Most are Muslim Arabs, although a few are Arab Christians. The remaining 17 percent of the inhabitants are Jews who have moved into the territory as part of Israel's program to settle the West Bank with new Israeli communities. All but a few of the

Gaza Strip's inhabitants are Palestinian Arabs; a small minority are Israeli military or business administrators.

In spite of the ongoing hostility between Jews and Arabs, the two groups are closely related. The Arabs and the original Jews were members of a larger group called the Semitic peoples, who trace their origins to Arabia and the southern part of the Middle East. Although the original Semitic group has long since split into many different nations and cultures, people of Semitic heritage share certain characteristics. For example, most are of medium height—slightly shorter than most Americans. They have dark brown or black hair, brown eyes, and skin ranging from a light-golden tan to medium brown. Because the Jewish people lived for centuries in Europe and other parts of the world, they have intermarried with people of other ethnic groups; it is not unusual to see Jewish Israelis with light hair and blue eyes.

The languages of the Israelis and the Arabs are related because they all originated in the same part of the world. Arabic and Hebrew (the Israeli language, which is based on the ancient Hebrew of the Bible) have some of the same words and sound similar to someone who does not speak either language; however, they are not so closely related that a Hebrew-speaker can understand Arabic, or the other way around.

Because the Arabs and the Israelis have lived side by side in Palestine for decades, many Israelis speak Arabic and some Arabs speak Hebrew. Although the Israeli government conducts its business in the West Bank and the Gaza Strip in Hebrew, the great majority of the population in both territories speaks Arabic. Most people in the territories follow traditional Arab customs regarding clothes, food, and family life. For example, many men, women, and children wear a garment that has not changed since biblical times: the *djellaba* (pronounced jell-AH-bah), a long, loose robe with long sleeves and a hood that is usually made of light-colored cloth for men and darker cloth for women. Sometimes men wear Western-style short-sleeved shirts and trousers under their djellabas. Arab women, however, rarely wear Western clothes.

Older Arab men often wear a headdress called a *kaffiyeh*. The kaffiyeh of the Palestinian Arabs is generally a white cloth with red or black checks, draped over the head like a loose scarf and held in place around the forehead by a small piece of braid. Sometimes, though, the kaffiyeh is wrapped around the head like a turban. Women keep their heads covered almost all of the time, usually with a turban or scarf of dark material. Palestinian Arab women, especially older women, may wear veils over their faces, even though their religion does not require them to do so.

Older Palestinian men wearing kaffiyehs and djellabas finger their worry beads.

The food of the Palestinian Arabs is very similar to that of most other North African and Middle Eastern peoples. Street vendors are popular, and the Palestinians often buy snacks or light meals from them while going about the day's business. They eat the main meal of the day between 2 P.M. and 3 P.M., and a smaller meal at night.

A favorite traditional dish is *mensaf*. Served at feasts and in honor of guests, it consists of a yard-wide (meter-wide) platter of rice, covered with pine nuts and a rich stew made from an entire lamb or goat. Other popular dishes include *musukhan* (boiled chicken with olive oil and spices), *yahkne* (a meat casserole with onions, cabbage, and tomatoes), and *mahsi* (vine leaves stuffed with chopped meat, onions, and rice). *Mazza*, a popular meal served to honor a guest, is an assortment of *hummus* (mashed chickpeas with lemon and garlic), sardines, tomatoes, cucumbers, pickles, and fried eggs.

The graceful curves of classical Arabic adorn the interior of a mosque.

Many Palestinian Arabs cannot afford to eat large, elaborate meals with lots of meat, and dine instead on *felafel* (sandwiches made with balls of deep-fried hummus), or *shwarma* (sandwiches of grilled lamb). Pastries, usually featuring honey and almonds or pistachio nuts, are also popular. Round, flat loaves of unleavened bread, called *pita*, are part of every meal.

Arabs drink a great deal of tea and coffee. Sometimes they follow a complex coffee-making ritual called the *gahwa sa' ada*. Roasted coffee beans are first ground in a carved wooden mortar and pestle known as a *mihbash*. Used almost like a musical instrument, the mihbash beats out a distinctive rhythm that tells friends and neighbors that coffee is being prepared. The ground beans are boiled in a brass pot, and then poured through cardamom pods (a strongly flavored spice) into a smaller pot. Finally, the brew is poured through twigs into a small pot, from which it is served. The coffee cups are also small; a guest can drain a cup in two or three sips, but his host will refill the cup many times. Coffee or tea drinking is an important part of social activity for Arab men. Most conversations or business deals conclude with several cups of either coffee or tea.

Men occupy a central position in Arab family life. The oldest man of the family makes all decisions involving money, living arrangements, and his children's marriages. Obedience to a father or a husband is one of the most honored values of Arab life; most young men and women would never question an older man's authority.

Arab men can have as many as four wives, but most Palestinians have only one or two. If a man has two wives and can afford a large house, he gives each wife a complete set of rooms for herself. In most cases, however, houses consist of only two or three rooms, and family members do not expect much privacy. Families tend to live together in the same household, and it is quite rare for young people to have homes of their own before they are married and have children. Even married children often live with the husband's parents.

Palestinian folk arts include woven rugs and tapestries, leather goods, pottery, and ceramic jars, bowls, and cups. The religion of Islam forbids the portrayal of people or animals, so most Arab designs feature plants, leaves, or geometric shapes such as stripes.

Arabs value courtesy and hospitality, and they like to share family and religious festivals. Songs, ballads, and stories enliven feasts and holidays, especially in the small villages, where the people have special songs for weddings, births, plowing, harvesting, and other events of daily life. Palestinians also enjoy dances called *debkah*, in which the dancers pound their feet on the ground to mark the rhythm.

Communications and Organizations

Poverty and unsettled political conditions have kept the West Bank and Gaza Strip Palestinians from developing their own movie and

Muslims believe that Muhammad ascended to heaven from the site of the Dome of the Rock mosque in Jerusalem.

book-publishing industries. Books and movies are imported, mainly from Arab countries. The most popular books and films are about Arab history, although some younger Palestinians also enjoy adventure films made in the United States and Japan.

Many Palestinian writers and artists now live outside the territories as exiles. Their work often deals with contemporary politics and the plight of the Palestinians. One of the best-known works by a Palestinian is the poem "Identity Card" by Mahmoud Darwish, which dramatically captures the Palestinians' dilemma:

> Record!
> I am an Arab
> without a name—without title
> patient in a country
> with people enraged
>
> I do not hate man
> Nor do I encroach
> But if I become hungry
> The usurper's flesh will be my food
> Beware—beware—of my hunger
> and my anger!

The works of Edward Said have also become well known. Many of his books, such as *Peace and Its Discontents*, explore the problems and hopes of the Palestinian people. Born in Palestine in 1935, Said came to the United States as a student and later became a distinguished faculty member at Columbia University.

Most Palestinians in the West Bank and the Gaza Strip own inexpensive radios. They listen to broadcasts in Arabic from other countries and from local stations. Locally published Palestinian newspapers and small magazines also circulate widely among the Arabs in the territories. The most popular paper is *Al-Fajr*, published daily in East Jerusalem.

Until recently, all newspapers and magazines in the West Bank and Gaza had to be approved by an Israeli board of censors. If a newspaper chose to print a story that had not been submitted to the censors for approval, the paper's distribution could be banned for a month or more. Israel also restricted the importation of printed matter from Jordan and other countries.

Palestinian journalists did not take the censorship mildly. They complained that it violated their right to a free press. The Israelis countered that many of the Palestinian papers were supported by organizations that participated in guerrilla activities and called for the overthrow of Israel. According to the Israelis, censorship was necessary to prevent the Palestinian press from becoming a threat to Israel's security.

Besides newspapers and periodicals, Palestinians have a number of other cultural organizations, mostly concentrated in East Jerusalem. They include a national theater, two music schools, and various museums. Outside Jerusalem, there are few theaters, museums, or recreational societies. However, cultural centers in Ramallah and Nablus help provide enrichment for children and adults. For example, the Popular Arts Center in Ramallah offers choir, painting, drama, and puppet-making to children from poor backgrounds. The center's top priority is to protect Palestinian folklore, especially tales, music, and songs. The Small Hands Association in Nablus teaches art and computer skills to children. Unfortunately, funds for equipment and staff at such cultural centers are often in short supply.

Land of Three Faiths

The people living on the West Bank and the Gaza Strip practice three religions: Islam, Judaism, and Christianity. Muslims are the largest group, and as a result the territories are essentially Muslim lands where Islamic practices shape daily life.

Like Judaism and Christianity, Islam is a monotheistic religion, meaning that Muslims recognize only one god, whom they call Allah. Muslims believe that Muhammad, who founded Islam, was the most recent in a series of prophets that included Abraham, Moses, and Jesus—the same biblical figures who appear in the Jewish and Christian religions. Muhammad set forth the word of Allah in the Koran, the Islamic holy book. The Koran outlines not only the religious doctrines to be followed by Muslims but also provides rules for government and everyday behavior.

Nearly all Palestinian Muslims are Sunni Muslims, members of the largest subgroup, or sect, within Islam. The Sunnis are orthodox Muslims, which means that most Muslims recognize Sunni beliefs and practices as the true version of Islam. But there are many smaller sects within Islam. The largest of these sects is the Shiite. Shiite Muslims make up about one-tenth of the world's Muslim population. The Shiites separated from orthodox Islam in the late 7th century. Shiites believe that only the descendants of Ali, who was Muhammad's son-in-law and the fourth caliph of the Arab Empire, may serve as *imams* (spiritual leaders). They refuse to participate in the elections by which Sunni Muslims choose their imams.

Most Shiite Muslims live in Iran, Iraq, southern Lebanon, and parts of Yemen, Turkey, Syria, and northern India. The Shiites and Sunnis have often been violently hostile to one another, because each sect believes its interpretation of Islam to be correct. In recent years, Arab states with Sunni leaders have faced growing unrest among Shiites, who have called for governments to rule according to the Shiite version of Islam.

Many Islamic customs and festivals are part of Arab life. Devout Muslims kneel and pray five times each day, either in public or in private. When they pray, they bow in the direction of the Saudi Arabian city of Mecca, the birthplace of the prophet Muhammad. *Muezzins* (criers) announce the times for prayer from high towers known as minarets. The skylines of the West Bank and the Gaza Strip are punctuated by the low round domes of the mosques (Muslim places of worship) and the pointed spires of the minarets.

Friday is the holy day of the week for Muslims. Many shops and businesses close on Friday, and most Muslims pray together at their neighborhood mosques. Daily prayer and weekly mosque attendance are two of what Muslims call the "five pillars" of faith. The other three pillars are giving money (alms) to the poor, making at least one pilgrimage to Mecca, and fasting during certain religious holidays.

The biggest religious holiday is Ramadan, the ninth month of the Islamic year. During Ramadan Muslims are forbidden to eat, drink, or transact business between sunrise and sunset. Everyone looks forward to the evening, when they eat large meals and decorate houses and trees with candles and lanterns. Many people stay up quite late, eating and praying. The last day of Ramadan is known as Id al-Fitr (festival of breaking the fast), and ends in a joyous *iftar*, or evening feast.

Another important Muslim holiday is Id al-Adha (festival of sacrifice), which honors the Old Testament prophet Abraham. It lasts for four days and usually occurs in the fall. Sheep are slaughtered and cooked according to traditional recipes, and families and friends join in a lively festival.

Probably no more than 100,000 of the West Bank Arabs are Christian. Some are the descendants of Arabs who converted to Christianity centuries ago. Like Christians everywhere, they celebrate Sunday as the Sabbath, or holy day. They worship in Roman Catholic, Greek Orthodox. Anglican, or Lutheran churches, most of which are located in Jerusalem.

The Jews who live in the West Bank make up the third religious group in the territories. They worship in synagogues and celebrate the Sabbath on Saturday. In towns where members of three faiths

Two tall minarets dominate the mosque at the Cave of Machpelah, which is believed to hold the remains of biblical figures revered by Jews, Christians, and Muslims alike. In 1994, after a tragic massacre at the mosque, Arabs and Jews agreed to visit it at separate times.

live side by side, the same communities often observe three separate holy days: Friday for Muslims, Saturday for Jews, and Sunday for Christians.

The West Bank and the Gaza Strip contain places and buildings that are sacred to each of the three religions. Muslims associate these holy sites with the tradition of Muhammad's visit to Jerusalem and with the Islamic conquest of Palestine. Jews associate them with the prophets, patriarchs, and kings who appear in the Old Testament. And Christians associate them with events in the life and death of Jesus.

The Old City of Jerusalem, still considered by many Palestinians to be rightfully part of the West Bank, contains many of Palestine's holiest places, including the Christian church called the Holy Sepulchre, the Muslim mosque called the Dome of the Rock, and the Jewish shrine called the Wailing Wall. Bethlehem, to the south of Jerusalem in the West Bank, is revered by Christians as the birthplace of Christ. It has the Christian Church of the Nativity and several convents. It also has a small, ancient building believed by Jews to be the tomb of Rachel, one of the heroines of the Old Testament.

In some cases, more than one religion regards the same building as holy. Disputes over who should control these holy places is one source of conflict among followers of the different faiths.

An example of religious conflict can be found in the West Bank city of Hebron. Jews, Muslims, and Christians alike believe that a local cave called the Cave of Machpelah holds the bodies of many revered Old Testament figures, including Abraham, Isaac, and even Adam and Eve. Because some of these figures are sacred to all three religions, believers have fought over the site for many centuries. During King Solomon's reign, the Jews built a temple above the Cave of Machpelah. Since then, however, the cave has changed hands several times. Christians of the Byzantine Empire built a small chapel there in the 5th or 6th century A.D., and Muslim conquerors added a mosque in the 7th century. Christian crusaders from Europe captured Hebron in 1103 and turned the mosque into a church. Less than a century later, the Ottoman Turks drove them out and rebuilt the mosque, complete with two tall minarets.

Today, the enormous rambling building over the cave is still a Muslim mosque, but the Israelis insist that the Muslims must make it available to Jews and Christians as well (except during the Islamic hours of prayer). The mosque was the target of a tragic massacre in 1994. An Israeli doctor, living in a West Bank settlement, opened fire on worshipers. Israeli forces stepped up security after Hebron was turned over to Palestinian administration, but tension remained high. When violence flares, the site is temporarily closed to visitors. An agreement was reached for Israelis and Arabs to visit the sacred place at different times to reduce the risk of disturbance.

A West Bank family discusses its problems with a United Nations worker. Unlike the people of the Gaza Strip, most West Bank Palestinians live in their original homes.

Life in the West Bank

The West Bank has never been a wealthy region. It has traditionally been a land of small farms, pastures, and quiet towns and villages. The economy is still based on agriculture. The chief farm crops are grains, fruit and vegetables, and above all olives, which grow on half of the cultivated land. In the north, sheep are raised for their wool and meat. The supply of water varies from one area to the next, and the amount dictates how the land can best be used.

Though most of the region is rural, the major towns of Janin, Nablus, and Ramallah lie to the north of Jerusalem, and the ancient cities of Bethlehem and Hebron, which are both tourist favorites, are to the south. The chief town in the Jordan River valley is Jericho, another ancient religious site. Most industrial activity takes place in and near the urban areas and in the western part of the region, close to Israeli-built roads and markets.

In 1988, after Jordan gave up control of the West Bank, Israel claimed the right to administer all the land in the territory that was neither cultivated nor privately owned. More recently, under the interim stages of self-government established by the peace process, Palestinians have taken on the responsibility of education, health, tourism, and taxation They have also developed a judicial system and police force. Some responsibilities are shared with the United Nations Relief and Works Agency (UNRWA), which meets most refugee needs. There are still over half a million refugees in the West Bank, about a third of them living in camps.

UNRWA provides health, educational, training, and social services, as well as money for the needy who are unemployed. The

agency staffs over 30 health centers and a small hospital, providing free basic health care to hundreds of thousands of refugees. There are also services to help special groups such as the elderly and people with disabilities.

Many Jewish Israelis live in the West Bank, especially since the wave of new settlements began in the 1990s. Their homes are gener-

A Palestinian rides his donkey along a road overlooking the West Bank town of Halhul.

ally segregated from Palestinian communities, and the Palestinians resent the fact that the best roads and services cater mainly to the settlers. Some Jewish settlements are self-contained farming communities. Others consist of huge apartment buildings that ring East Jerusalem, with jobs and shopping facilities close at hand.

As the reins of West Bank government are handed over to the Palestinian leadership, Israelis have continued to provide security in and around the region to protect people from terrorist attacks. Some Palestinians argue that if there were no Israeli presence, there would be no terrorism. When attacks are threatened or carried out, the Israelis have responded by closing the borders.

Such closures hinder thousands of West Bank Palestinians who cross into Israel to work each day. Over the years, an increasing number of work permits have been granted to Palestinians, and their earnings contribute an important sum to the West Bank economy. Palestinians working for Israel participate in the country's national social security scheme, though their benefits are limited. Currency in the West Bank is the same as in Israel, the new Israeli shekel.

Companies are small in the West Bank, often employing fewer than ten people. Little vocational training has been available. For many generations, the people of the region have been renowned for handicrafts like mother-of-pearl items, textiles, and ceramics. Newer light industries include jewelry and diamond cutting, electronics, and the manufacture of toys, plastic goods, furniture, clothing, and shoes. Businesses often find it difficult to establish substantial markets, because for many years most products have gone to Israel rather than to outlets farther afield. At present, the region has no railroads, and the roads are insufficient to transport a large volume of products. The territory has only two small airports.

Most families in the West Bank are large and live in overcrowded homes. Almost half the population is under fifteen years of age. Many homes now have television, and most have radios. About one in ten households has a telephone. In the rural parts of the West Bank, only about half the homes have electricity available around the clock, but the situation is better in the towns.

Education is a high priority in the West Bank. All children attend primary school, and there are several institutions of higher education, including universities and community colleges. The best known is Birzeit University, which has about 5,000 students and faculty.

Perhaps in part because jobs are hard to come by and unemployment figures are very high, many Palestinian men still consider it unacceptable for women to work outside the home. Even more think that Western dress is inappropriate for women. They prefer the traditional garments that are less revealing. These attitudes affect education as well: by the time students reach the ninth grade, more girls than boys have dropped out. Despite this, young women (but not older ones), have a higher literacy rate than young men, and 40 percent of the university students are women.

Beach Camp, pictured above, is one of the many Palestinian refugee camps located in the Gaza Strip. After half a century of existence, the camp has become a permanent settlement.

Life in the Gaza Strip

The Gaza Strip has more problems than the West Bank. Until war shattered the region in 1948, it was not destined to become home to almost a million people. The land has few natural resources, and most of the population has no sense of belonging there.

Nearly three-fourths of the land is under cultivation, with most of the arable land lying in the southeast and central areas. Citrus crops are the mainstay of the agricultural economy, and the fruit is exported to European and other countries. Unfortunately, the future of the orchards is threatened because the salinity (saltiness) of the ground water is three times the level regarded safe by the World Health Organization. Besides the worsening quality of the water, there is also a growing shortage of water.

When times are peaceful, Gaza City and other spots in the north attract tourists. The handicrafts and small manufacturing plants mostly lie in this area, but only a handful of enterprises in the Gaza Strip employ more than four people. Fishing was once important, but Israeli restrictions and the need for modern equipment have reduced opportunities for profit.

The Gaza Strip is about nine times more densely populated than the West Bank, and the population is increasing at the rate of close to

8 percent per year. The latest figures show that over half the population is below the age of fifteen. There are over half a million refugees in the Gaza Strip—that is, over half of the current population are classified as refugees, and the majority of them still live in camps. Generally, these camps no longer fit the image of tents and temporary facilities; they look more like established towns. Still, the living conditions there are poor.

For almost twenty years, with a short break during the 1950s, the Gaza Strip was under Egyptian military rule. Egypt did not allow the refugees to become Egyptian citizens or to migrate to Egypt or other Arab countries. They were under the care of UNRWA, the United Nations Relief and Works Agency. The agency still shoulders much of the care and cost of the refugees. It runs several well-equipped health centers here, and two hospitals.

With such a fast-growing population, education is extremely important. The Egyptian system of schooling is still followed, but the administration of schools has shifted from the Israeli Civil Administration to the Palestinian Authority. There are two universities, a teacher

The United Nations provides health care for Palestinian children in the Gaza Strip.

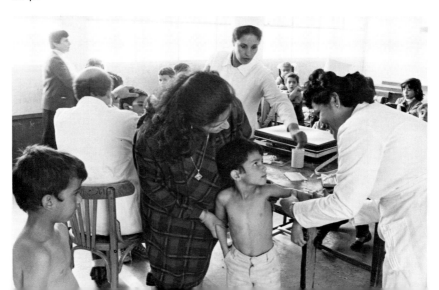

training college, and close to 30 literacy centers. Despite shortage of funds, some cultural centers have also been opened to enrich children and adults.

During the early years of Israeli occupation, a number of young people, especially boys, rebelled against the poor living conditions and became *fedayeen* (Arab guerrillas operating against Israel). Their attacks added to the problems confronting the region. The Israeli government retaliated by imposing extra security measures, and frequently by preventing Palestinian day laborers from crossing the border to work. At any particular time, almost half of the Gaza Strip's work force may be employed in Israel. When the border is closed, this means no work for many thousands of people. Egyptian employment laws still regulate employment conditions, but the system offers no pension benefits, compensation for work-related injuries, health insurance, or severance pay. Unemployment remains one of the Gaza Strip's central problems. Only about 25 percent of the men and 15 percent of the women are fully employed.

Few homes have telephones, but almost all have radios, and well over half now have televisions. Services like a reliable water supply, electricity, and sewerage need to be improved. Because roads are poor, and there is no railroad or airport, it is difficult to develop an economic base that includes exports beyond Israel. As a result of these difficulties, even when the goal of Palestinian independence is achieved, the Gaza Strip's problems will not easily be solved.

Palestinian children display a homemade Palestinian flag as they express their desire for a peaceful homeland.

An Uncertain Future

The West Bank and the Gaza Strip have been battlegrounds for thousands of years. Nation after nation has fought to control a land that has been coveted by many. Various groups of people began to settle the land about 1700 B.C. The Hebrews arrived in the 12th century B.C. They inhabited the region for centuries, building a flourishing kingdom under Solomon and David only to be driven from the land in the 2d century A.D. by the Roman Empire.

Roman rule lasted until the 4th century A.D., when Palestine (as it was then called) was conquered by the Persians and then by the Arab Muslims. The powerful Muslims ruled the land until 1917, when Great Britain defeated the Turkish Muslim forces holding Palestine.

Beginning in the 19th century, many Jews living in Europe decided that the only way to end their persecution was to build a Jewish homeland. These Jews formed a movement called Zionism, which encouraged Jewish migration to Palestine. As the Jews began to enter Palestine, the Arab inhabitants of the region felt increasingly threatened; riots and fighting between Arabs and Jews began to occur. Great Britain, which had assumed control of the region after World War I, complicated matters by promising Palestine to both the Jews and the Arabs. Hostilities worsened, and Great Britain turned the problem over to the United Nations, which divided the region into separate Jewish and Arab states. The Jews accepted this plan and established the nation of Israel in 1948.

The first of many wars immediately broke out when the surrounding Arab countries invaded the new state. At the war's end, Egypt gained control of the Gaza Strip and Jordan took over the West Bank. Thousands of Palestinian Arab refugees left Israel and poured into these territories and into other Arab nations. In 1967, Israel attacked the surrounding Arab countries. By the end of the Six-Day War, Israel had gained control of both the Gaza Strip and the West Bank.

In November 1967, the United Nations passed Resolution 242 calling for two immediate changes. The first was the withdrawal of Israeli troops from the territories they had occupied during the Six-Day War. The second part of the resolution called for recognition of Israel's right to exist as a sovereign state. For years, it seemed that neither side made serious efforts to comply. The 1973 Yom Kippur War and the brutal war in Lebanon in 1982 defied any attempts to create a lasting peace. With each outbreak of terrorist violence, the Israelis reinforced their troops in the occupied territories. It was not until 1988, more than 20 years after the Resolution was passed, that Yasir Arafat, as spokesman for the PLO, formally acknowledged Israel's political existence.

This gesture opened the door for a series of peace talks in the 1990s. The future, which had looked so bleak, now offered some hope. Yet thoughtful Palestinians and Israelis realized that many adjustments would need to be made. Beside the obvious ones, such as turning over administration of the territories to the Palestinians, a change in attitudes was needed. The two sides had to come to grips with each other's presence in the region and figure out ways to live at peace, if not in immediate friendship.

Palestinian children walk across the sand toward their house near Jabalah camp in Gaza City. Palestinian authorities plan to remove these shanty houses made of metal sheets and rehouse the residents in upgraded dwellings.

But there was more to be done. Even if peace plans stayed on track and the Palestinians finally gained an independent state, the region could not provide enough jobs and homes for the population. The number of Palestinians living in the West Bank and Gaza Strip had grown tremendously since the United Nations announced the decision to divide Palestine in 1947. By the late 1990s, several new industrial zones were being planned or constructed with foreign investment. It was clear, though, that even these new initiatives would not be able to provide enough jobs for all who needed them. Nor could agriculture continue to grow if the water supply kept deteriorating.

Today the Gaza Strip is still not a hospitable place. The Arabs who fled here did not expect this narrow strip of land to become their permanent home. True, the refugee camps—once tents without run-

ning water or electricity—have become more like regular neighbor-
hoods. But raising children there, even with the help of UNRWA, is
nobody's idea of a decent life.

The West Bank has more obvious potential for the future. Although the Israeli occupation has not brought enough roads and services to the territory, the land itself yields more opportunity than the
Gaza Strip. If foreign investors feel their money is in safe hands, industry and agriculture can expand. This region has been the home of
Palestinians, including the ancestors of many present families, for
thousands of years. There is a loyalty to the land.

Whatever the political situation, most people living in the West
Bank and Gaza Strip cannot spend their days thinking about it. They
go to school or work, cook and eat, watch television or listen to the
radio, play sports, enjoy the company of friends. When violence
erupts, the pattern of their daily life gives way to tragedy. They can
only hope that the political dilemmas will be resolved, the anger and
bitterness of many years will recede, and the region's long-term economic problems will be given some serious attention. At last this
dream, so long sought, seems within the realm of possibility.

‹ G L O S S A R Y ›

Debkah Palestinian dances in which the dancers mark the rhythm by pounding their feet on the ground.

Djellaba The traditional garment of Arab men and women: a long, loose robe with loose sleeves and a hood. It is usually made of light-colored cloth for men and darker cloth for women.

Fawakhyr An ancient factory in Gaza where pottery is handcrafted from the black clay of the Sinai Peninsula.

Felafel Sandwiches made with balls of deep-fried *hummus* (mashed chickpeas).

Fedayeen An Arab term meaning "commandos," usually used to refer to young men who join illegal anti-Israel organizations.

Iftar The evening feast that ends the month-long holiday of Ramadan.

Kaffiyeh An Arab man's headdress like a shawl or turban that is usually made of white cloth with red or black checks; it is held in place by a braided cord around the forehead.

Mahsi Vine leaves stuffed with chopped meat, onions, and rice.

Mazza An assortment of *hummus* (mashed, seasoned chickpeas), sardines, tomatoes, cucumbers, pickles, and fried eggs.

Mensaf	A traditional Palestinian dish of rice, pine nuts, and a stew made from a whole goat or lamb. Mensaf is often served at feasts or in honor of guests.
Mihbash	A carved wooden mortar and pestle used to grind roasted coffee beans.
Minaret	A tower from which the muezzin calls out the signals for Muslim prayers.
Monotheism	The belief in a single god rather than in many gods and goddesses.
Mosque	A Muslim place of worship, usually with a low, rounded dome.
Muezzin	A Muslim crier who chants out the call to prayers five times each day.
Musukhan	Boiled chicken with olive oil and spices.
Pita	Round, flat loaves of bread.
Ramadan	A month-long Islamic holiday during which Muslims are forbidden to eat, drink, or carry out any business during the daylight hours.
Shwarma	Sandwiches of grilled lamb.
Yahkne	A meat casserole with onions, cabbage, and tomatoes.

◄ I N D E X ►